https://nickarnett.net

Facebook: StressIntoStrength

YouTube: Stress Into Strength

Twitter: NickArnett

Eventbrite (training): http://stress_into_strength.eventbrite.com/

Email: nick.arnett+pandemicbook@gmail.com

D1472291

Resilience During the Pandemic

Nick Arnett

Dedication

This book is dedicated to all of those who give their lives for others, figuratively or literally. Those who serve – paid or volunteer; private or public; religious or secular – to keep our society functioning.

I especially remember friends and family that we lost too soon: my sister Susie, who lost her fight with ovarian cancer on May 9, 2020, my sister, Lesley, who died in the H1N1 epidemic that started in 2009; John Heidish, of Penn Hills Fire; Wes Canning of the United States Marine Corps; and Jimmy McCluskey, of Santa Clara County Fire.

Contents

Preface

I'm a firefighter, Emergency Medical Technician, and fire chaplain, with fifteen years of experience, providing and teaching crisis intervention, peer support and resilience, with first responders and the public. I've known the stresses of other careers, too: paramedic, journalist, co-owner of a market research company, software inventor and product manager. Like many others who do this work, I came into it as a client, after a line-of-duty death in my extended family.

After leading or participating in around a thousand interventions, for crises from personal to international, I developed a desire to learn about and teach what it is that makes us strong and resilient. Next year (though I am hoping it may be sooner), HarperCollins Leadership plans to release another book I am currently working on: *Stress into Strength: Resilience Routines for Warriors, Wimps and Everybody in Between*. The research and writing that I have been doing for that book has helped make it possible for me to produce this one rapidly.

I've had tremendous support from family, friends, mentors, and clients. My wife, Cindy, who served alongside me on some of those interventions, has allowed – if not supported – the disruptions to our lives that this work causes. She listens just as well as our two dogs do (that's a compliment; dogs are among the best listeners). Janet Childs, the leader of our Bay Area Critical Incident Stress Management Team and Director of Education at the Centre for Living with Dying, invited me to engage in this work after I was her client. In the decade and a half since then, she has been a comfort and inspiration to countless people and organizations. I've had the privilege of training with Jeff Mitchell and George Everly, founders of the International Critical Incident Stress Foundation, and pioneers of modern crisis intervention. K-Love Radio's free training, through their Crisis Response Care program, connected me with other outstanding instructors: K.C. Peterson, Naomi Pagett, Tina Brooks and Jennifer Ellers. Chief Jim Cook and the California Fire Chaplain Association helped me translate my skills into spiritual care and support. My home church for nearly forty years, Bethel Lutheran in Cupertino, California, has been a rock; without support from its pastors, leaders and congregation – along with Stephen Minister and my other training – I can't imagine where I would be. Retreats and groups run by Walk to Emmaus and Illuman's men's groups, along with Richard Rohr's leadership, have supplied more wisdom and support.

Cal Fire's Employee Support Services team, led in recent years by Bill Baxter, Bob Ellis, and Mike Ming, has been a privilege to work with, and I am always honored to be asked. The same goes for Santa Clara County Parks and Supervising Ranger Aniko Milan, who were the test subjects for my first resilience training classes. A big thanks to Mike Hacke and Jerry Serpa, Spring Valley Fire Department chiefs, for bringing me on board and maintaining high standards of training and performance; that has also been a privilege.

Two guys I regularly "get real" with, Dave Land and Dave Hibbert, have helped keep me sane by sharing a couple of thousand meals over the last few decades. I'm also grateful to my mentors, coaches, investors, and encouragers, especially Bruce Dobler, Tim Bajarin, John Lemons, Gary Kalus and David Brin. Toastmasters taught me more than I expected, so a thank-you also to James Gardner, for dragging me to the Early Risers meeting. Meanwhile, Margot Maley Hutchinson, my literary agent at Waterside Associates, has been a source of honest feedback and encouragement. And, I am always grateful to my parents, for choosing to live in a town with an outstanding public-school system.

Please feel free to contact me at the email address on the copyright page of this book. I welcome your feedback, corrections, and suggestions for improving future editions.

Chapter 1:

Our New Normal

Fear, worry, blame and anxiety are natural responses to threats, especially when reliable information is scarce, and uncertainty is high. If you are finding it hard to believe that current events are actually happening, as if you are living in a movie, then know that you are not alone. Nearly everybody, even medical disaster professionals, are feeling that same way, at least some of the time: "Is this really happening?"

Our world and our lives won't ever be the same again. Even though the crisis looks as if it will last a long time, it is only temporary; things will eventually become better. Goodness will continue to happen, alongside the difficult bits, but it is hard to acknowledge that right now. The world has become extraordinarily unpredictable, while control and information are hard to come by. That's a formula for high stress, indeed.

If you have found yourself stuffing down fears, tears, anger or other difficult feelings about what's happening, including around the possibility that you or those you care about may get sick or die, that's perfectly normal. If you are worried about a possible breakdown of basic social order, that's normal, too (though unlikely; only a tiny percentage of people behave badly during a disaster). Are you sometimes mad at people who aren't following health guidelines or orders? Completely normal. Looking for someone to blame? Normal. Angry and sad that life has changed so tremendously; perhaps angry at God, for allowing this? Those are also very normal reactions to a world which suddenly became so abnormal. You are not alone if you are frustrated and tired, exhausted even, by how unrelenting this emergency sometimes feels.

These reactions are normal results of the activation of your brain's stress autopilot, which can take over your thoughts, emotions, and actions in an instant. It doesn't just react to danger; it also activates when it senses that you are taking on a challenge or are presented with an opportunity. People sometimes call this your "monkey mind," because it cares little about logic. It is your friend when you need to rise to an occasion or deal with danger, but the more it activates and the longer it stays active, the stickier it is. And, when it is stuck, you have a hard time living in the present moment, because it is reacting to things which happened in the past (anxiety), or rehearsing (worrying about) what might happen in the future.

Being stuck in a stress reaction will wear you out.

Negative Bias

The global situation is bad and, at the time of writing this, looks like it will get worse. But, it is important to keep in mind that our brains urge us to react more strongly to negative information. When we become aware of a risk or a threat, we are much more likely to believe it, act on it, worry about it and share it with others. Although this "negative bias" has helped us to survive and thrive, news media, politicians and others often play on it to get our attention — because it works.

You can begin to counteract your negative bias by changing your mindset. When you begin to get cabin fever from being stuck at home, recall that you are in a safe place. When you worry about getting sick, remind yourself of the things that you are doing to stay healthy (staying at home; washing your hands, disinfecting surfaces, etc.). When you worry about running out of something, remind yourself that you have everything that you need right now. When it bothers you that so many places are closed, remind yourself that the important ones are still open: grocery stores, gas stations, pharmacies, and hospitals. When helplessness and lack of control over your life raise your anxiety, consider what you can and do control: diet, exercise, contact with those who you care about and spiritual practices. These good thoughts cannot erase your worries, but they do help to *balance* them, keeping your "monkey mind" from taking charge so much.

Disaster movies, the news and other media exaggerate how often people panic, riot, loot or generally misbehave during disasters, but although some of that does happen, it is actually quite rare. Yet, it will make headlines. In reality, nearly everyone reacts by cooperating, looking after each other and doing what is best for their community, rather than behaving entirely selfishly.

I went to Haiti with a medical team, following the 2010 earthquake. In a place like that, with almost no functioning government, millions living underneath sheets held up by sticks, and not even enough food and water, you might think that there would be a lot of selfishness, looting, violence and so forth. But, there wasn't. Admittedly, there was a little, and some short tempers - we had to be careful, because people were desperate, and we didn't go out at night – but nearly everybody was cooperative, surprisingly patient, helpful to one another and more. In even the worst disasters, people behave much better than we often imagine. The bad actors get a lot of attention, so it is important to remember that very few people react in this way.

Typical Reactions

As a disaster unfolds, here are the ways in which people usually react:

Pre-disaster: This is when you know something bad may be imminent; perhaps there has been a tornado warning, or you hear that there are going to be layoffs at work, which might include you. People feel vulnerable, fearful, and uncertain; they might feel guilty or angry, as if they should have somehow been more prepared. Most of us are beyond this point in the current pandemic.

Impact: As things unfold, disbelief and shock are often followed by concern for one's own safety and that of loved ones. If you are feeling this way, you are far from alone.

Heroic: Immediately after disaster strikes, people are grateful and supportive toward those who are responding directly to the threat. At the beginning of the Covid-19 disaster, people were calling out medical and first responder personnel, who were preparing for and starting to deal with huge numbers of very sick people. People sometimes take big risks to help strangers in immediate danger.

Honeymoon: As time passes, people's shock diminishes, and they are better able to adjust to the changes. They can see that resources are being mobilized; many people pitch in to help. It begins to feel like we are all going to bond more closely together and emerge better and stronger at the end.

Disillusionment: As the stress builds, people start to become tired, cranky, irritable, and impatient, as the stress continues, but opportunities to rest and recover are scarce. The limits of disaster relief start to become apparent, and now nobody seems to be doing enough; criticism is launched back and forth. Now, it starts to seem like rather than coming together in triumph, it is all falling apart.

Reconstruction: Eventually, the disaster is over – although, the pandemic may take a long time to end, and the effects will last far longer. Over time, we will feel less like victims of the virus and begin to rebuild our lives. Then, one day we will wake up and realize that the "new normal" is just normal. We are recovering and we will be okay.

Like the phases of grief, hardly anyone goes through these stages in order. People, including yourself, will bounce around among them; the recovery process looks more like spaghetti than a straight line. Expect those around you to react differently than you, than each other, and on a different schedule. Be patient with all people, including yourself. Remember, beneath our individual reactions, we each have this in common: we are all ordinary people, struggling to cope with an overwhelming situation.

Although people are still like most other people, the Covid-19 pandemic isn't like most other disasters, making it hard to predict how we will react. It is more accurate to call this a catastrophe, rather than a disaster, because in many cases those we would ordinarily turn to for help in a disaster aren't available; they are struggling with their own difficulties, with little left over to spare.

If you find this scary and depressing at times, you aren't alone – far from it. You are experiencing a normal reaction, to a world which has become very abnormal.

Despite – or, perhaps because – of what's happening now, it is a time to be kinder, gentler and more patient with everyone, including ourselves.

Why do People Believe in Conspiracy Theories?

Conspiracy theories can offer a sense of control, reducing our threat response, when helplessness feels overwhelming.

For example, if the current pandemic came from a random virus mutation, then we had no control over it. But, if it was designed in a laboratory (conspiracy theory), then someone did have control over it. When we feel like somebody has – or could have had – control, our brain's stress autopilot calms down. The appeal of this is never about what we *think*, but about what we *feel*, in our gut.

Helplessness, lack of control and the inability to do anything about a perceived risk all trigger a *threat* response; a stronger stress reaction than that which applies to ordinary challenges. Conspiracy theories mitigate the stress by making people feel as if we are not – or, were not – entirely helpless. Even when reflecting on the past, if it feels as if somebody *could* have done something to stop the threat, that's reassuring, because our stress autopilot is always planning and rehearsing for future risks, based on past experiences.

Where is God? Is this Punishment?

Whenever something happens which sickens, injures, or kills many people, religious explanations pop up: "God is punishing us for X," or "God is punishing them for Y." The Bible and other holy writings all feature stories of God sending plagues and other disasters to punish people, but no one can be certain that's what is going on right now.

Like conspiracy theories, the idea that Covid-19 is a punishment appeals to our stress autopilot's desire for control and predictability. If it is a punishment, it means that we could prevent future plagues by improving our behavior - this gives us control and predictability of the future.

It is natural to struggle with why God would *allow* so much suffering and death. That is not a new question; people have wrestled with it through the ages. Doctrine typically explains that disease and death are consequences of free will. Talk to your religious leaders if you are struggling with these kinds of questions, but rest assured that it is entirely normal to have such thoughts and struggle with your faith when terrible events occur.

A more comforting vision of God can also be found in holy writings: A God who accompanies us in our suffering, who sheds tears alongside us. Many people believe in a *redemptive* God, who can make all things, even the worst, work for good. That is a good way to think about stress because – as you will learn in the next chapter – when stress is combined with rest, nutrition and recovery, its negative effects can be healed and transformed into strength, resilience and wisdom.

If you believe in God, possibly the most difficult feeling is wondering if God has abandoned you. Feeling isolated and alone magnifies stress enormously. If that is where you are at, talking to other believers and religious leaders can help, provided that they are the kind of people who will not try to "correct" you, but will acknowledge that such feelings are normal and difficult, while accompanying you in your struggle to find meaning. Reading stories of God's role in comforting the afflicted can help to reassure you. The Christian Bible has the words *"Don't be afraid"* hundreds of times, and on many of those occasions are followed by the reassurance *"...for I am with you."* The feeling of abandonment is temporary, although very real when you have it.

Why So Many Rumors?

We become more tribal under stress. Rumors and gossip, as poisonous as they are, bond people by emphasizing that "we" are not like "them;" anything which helps to distinguish our tribe from everybody else increases our sense of security. Your stress autopilot urges you to distrust strangers and become more generally suspicious, if hesitant to trust at all.

Like the conspiracy theories, rumors are also often related to our hunger for a sense that *somebody* has, or had, control.

Some rumors are simply motivated by the desire for attention, and to provoke outrage or dissent. But, still the common element is control versus helplessness.

Chapter 2:

Stress into Strength

Some people wake up in the morning, determined to take on a lot of stress. Crazy, huh?

And, you are probably one of them.

You might not consider yourself as *choosing* stress, but that's exactly what you are doing, each time you decide to go to the gym, fast, eat better, study for a test, prepare for an important meeting, be vulnerable with others, make a "stretch" donation or contribution, teach, coach, or anything else which takes you out of your comfort zone.

Isn't all that stress wearing us down?

Nope. Exercise, fasting, studying, intimacy, generosity, sharing knowledge or wisdom... these are all strength *builders*... if (and, it is the *big* if) you finally return to your comfort zone, for rest, relaxation, nourishment, companionship and contemplation. That's what this little book is all about: combining stress and recovery, to build strength and resilience.

We are living in stressful times, indeed. But, stress doesn't deserve its bad reputation. To grow strong and resilient, you *need* stress – physical, mental, and spiritual stress – with downtime for recovery, rebuilding and growth. Everyone knows this is true of muscles; the stress of exercise, at regular intervals, combined with rest and nutrition, makes them stronger and gives you greater endurance. And, when you are in shape, you bounce back faster from exertion. That's resilience. The same is true for mental and spiritual stress and recovery: without stress, living things would never adapt, develop, or grow.

Never think of yourself as a machine, like a car which wears down a little, every time you use it. Unlike a machine, when you get the right combination of exercise, rest and nourishment, the "wear" on your body, mind and spirit doesn't merely heal you; it can actually *increase* your strength, horsepower and endurance – even after an injury! The ability to transform stress and recovery into strength, flexibility and resilience is part of the miracle of living things.

I am using the words "spirit" and "spiritual" to refer to your values, ethics, priorities and sense of purpose; thoughts and feelings which are rooted less in logic and more in love, compassion and right-or-wrong. For many people, religion is a primary source of spiritual practices and beliefs.

The most harmful way to look at stress is unfortunately quite common: the myth of "toxic" stress. In truth, recent research shows that the *fear* of stress, rather than stress itself, negatively affects health. In a large study of American adults, those who reported high stress, but did not believe it was bad for them, lived the longest. Those who absorbed the myth of toxic stress were the quickest to die.

Stress plus recovery yields strength. For example, when you lift weights, your "fight or flight" response activates – but, you keep going anyway, if you're aiming for strength. When you also activate physical recovery ("rest and digest"), you build stronger muscles, bones, and cardiovascular fitness; you become stronger at *doing things.*

When you are transparent and vulnerable with others, your social stress reaction is to feel as if you need to "defend and distance" yourself – but, if you are aiming for stronger relationships, you keep going. Combining social exercise with social recovery ("tend and befriend") makes you *mentally stronger.*

When your values and ethics are challenged, your spiritual stress reaction is to become more "selfish and survivalist" – and, if you are aiming for stronger character, you tough it out. Combining spiritual exercise with spiritual recovery ("pause and plan") gives you a stronger sense of purpose and priority.

	Stress Response	Recovery Response	Strength
Physical	Fight or Flight	Rest and Digest	Doing
Social	Defend or Distance	Tend and Befriend	Thinking, Feeling
Spiritual	Selfish or Survivalist	Pause and Plan	Purpose, Priorities

Just like in weightlifting, stress can cause injury if you take on too much, do so too often, or fail to get enough rest and nutrition. You can also hurt yourself by taking on others' stress for them - furthermore, they won't grow stronger, and by taking on their "weights" you'll lift too much, with little energy left over to do your own lifting. Right now, as the pandemic weighs on our minds, it can be hard to take breaks, especially mental ones, so you may find yourself surprisingly tired, even when you are less active than usual. That's a result of being stuck in a stress reaction. The biggest part of building resilience is making your stress reaction less sticky.

Even though it is helpful to think about the physical, mental, and spiritual domains independently, your body, mind and spirit are inseparable. For example, although it might seem like a workout is purely physical, you need emotional strength to stick with exercise, despite feeling tired; you need spiritual strength to stay inspired and motivated, to go back and do it again and again. All resilience routines help in all three dimensions. The more you do them, the easier it becomes to make them habits, because as you calm your stress autopilot, the parts of your brain responsible for self-discipline and motivation are in charge more often.

As you read about the kind of habits which give you greater strength to cope with and bounce back from adversity, you will see that our culture has lost many of them in recent decades. We have become more disconnected from ourselves, nature, social support and the sources of wisdom and values – the very things which turn stress into strength. In other words, most of us are not getting enough opportunities to "rest and digest," "tend and befriend," or "pause and plan."

Although it is clear that dealing with the pandemic will be a marathon for humanity as a whole, individually we can only survive and thrive by treating it as a series of sprints, alternating intervals of stress and recovery. Your *downtime* is essential, but more easily postponed or forgotten, especially when you are feeling overwhelmed. Too many of us are treating ourselves like machines, refueling regularly, but not getting the downtime and connection-building which activate the wondrous ability of living things to rebuild, and grow from stress and recovery.

If all of this is sounding strange and questionable, consider these examples of how intervals of appropriate stress and recovery cause increased strength:

- The stress of fasting for short periods improves health and extends your life span;
- Growing evidence shows that small doses of ionizing radiation, generally seen as deadly, actually reduce cancer, by "toughening" your cells;
- Low doses of sunlight build protection from skin cancer (but you should still use sunscreen!);
- The stress of a cold shower gives some of the same benefits as intense exercise;

- Alternating guitar practice with rest is the only way to grow the tough fingertips which make it possible to play well without injury;
- Education is stressful – the resulting skills and knowledge make you stronger and more resilient;
- Conifer forests cannot reproduce without the stress of fire. Therefore, in the western United States, decades of fire suppression – a lack of stress – has weakened millions of trees, leaving them susceptible to beetles and catastrophic fires;
- Vaccines and low exposure to microbes trigger protection by stressing your immune system, triggering production of antibodies which will protect you against a larger exposure (let's hope this is true of Covid-19).

The idea that stress becomes strength isn't new. Consider these oft-repeated bits of wisdom: necessity is the mother of invention; no pain, no gain; adversity builds character; pain is weakness leaving the body; what doesn't kill you makes you stronger... Stress really can become strength.

Chapter 3:

Resilience Routines

Exercise, rest, and nourishment will only make you stronger if you practice them regularly. This is true of physical, mental, and spiritual exercise, recovery, and strength. Resilience routines are habits which trigger your body, mind, and spirit to grow stronger.

You are already naturally doing some of these; this book's goal is to help you become more aware and intentional about the habits which build strength, through regular challenges and recovery.

New habits? I don't stick with new habits.

It's not about sticking with them. You won't. Nobody does, consistently.

Here's the good news: you don't have to. Even Olympic athletes and Navy SEALs skip practice sometimes – and, this book is for ordinary, not exceptional, people. If you skip a routine, *start over.* Try again. There is no deadline. This isn't work or school, so nobody is grading you... except you – and, judging yourself is a self-defeating habit. Have compassion for yourself; practice being as kind to yourself as you would be with a struggling friend. Small successes become large ones, over time.

Forming new habits is simple, but not easy. Resist the temptation to try to do too much at once; start small and increase slowly. Break down big tasks into smaller ones. Let these two instructions guide you:

Start small.

Start over.

Building strength and resilience requires willpower, motivation, impulse control, perspective, and flexibility – but those are in short supply when you are feeling stressed! That's why *"Start Small; Start Over"* is essential. Just as you can *temporarily* lift too much weight in the gym, you can easily fool yourself into thinking you can make big changes rapidly, but you are almost certain to exhaust, and probably injure, yourself.

The pattern for all resilience routines is a lot like building strength in the gym:

- Establish safety;
- Get outside of your comfort zone – increase gradually;
- Pay attention to your technique and results;
- Wait the right amount of time between sets and workouts;
- Track your progress;
- Get rest and nutrition;
- When you don't keep to your schedule, start over.

The chapters which follow describe resilience routines in more detail, but this is a quick overview. Think of them as connecting activities in a very disconnected world. We grow and get energy from literal connections (physical) to each other (social), and to wisdom and values (spiritual).

Obstacles to Building Routines

Forget about using "time management" (which is really about willpower and self-discipline) to build resilience routines; that is a short-term solution, at best. Instead, think about managing and investing your *energy*.

The biggest obstacles are emotional – particularly guilt and shame, which backfire because they activate your stress response, taking more energy than they give. Begin letting go of your *"shoulds."* You know the "shoulds": you *should* eat better; you *should* exercise more, you *should* be more patient, you *should* spend less money, and so on...

A simple antidote to the "shoulds" is this: be gentle with yourself, as Janet Childs, my crisis intervention team leader, has taught so many of us.

That's worth repeating:

Be gentle with yourself.

You deserve at least as much compassion for yourself as you give to other people.

Letting go of "shoulds" has nothing to do with right and wrong; you should still do the right thing. I'm talking about the kind of "shoulds" which leave you feeling anxious, guilty, or ashamed. In fact, the word "should" is itself derived from ancient terms for guilt and owing money!

Feeling guilt or shame is natural. In fact, there is a name for those who lack the conscience which gives rise to these emotions: *psychopaths*. Accept what you are feeling, but don't let it tell you who you really are. Remind yourself that guilt is a message, that the true *you* knows that something is wrong.

Guilt and shame might seem to work in the short term, but because they are based in stress and fear, they will erode your motivation, enthusiasm, and self-discipline. To grow, you need periodic freedom from them.

Procrastination is often our favorite way to avoid feeling guilt and shame when we should – but, then we inevitably feel guilty about procrastinating! As Admiral Ackbar exclaimed, in *Star Wars: Episode VI:* "It's a trap!"

As you aspire to let go of your "shoulds", avoid generalizing, which has the terrible effect of turning guilt *("I did something bad")* into shame *("I am bad")*. Convert them into something positive. Be specific and include the *why*. In the long term, positive goals are far more powerful than guilt. For example, instead of saying *"I should get more exercise,"* try saying *"I will go to the gym today, so that I feel more energy and stay healthy."*

When you notice that a "should" is sneaking up on you, try substituting it with the words "choose" or "want." For example, instead of *"I should exercise today,"* try *"I choose (or want) to exercise today."*

One of the healthy habits especially important during a pandemic is to avoid touching your face. Instead of thinking *"I shouldn't touch my face"* (which often backfires, by triggering guilt or shame, which weaken self-control, when you inevitably fail), make it a positive resolve: *"By not touching my face, I'm staying healthier."* This is a small change, which makes a big difference. Do the same when giving other people, such as children, guidance. Instead of commanding "Wash your hands! Don't touch your face!" say things like "By not touching your face, you'll reduce your chances of getting sick."

If you do realize that you've just touched your face, perhaps before you washed your hands, remind yourself that even though you broke a health "rule", the odds that you just gave yourself the virus are still quite low. Don't let your stress autopilot, which is very judgmental, take charge.

Another way of thinking about the positive approach is that you are making it safe to fail, which makes it far easier to start over. We all need to start over, sometimes.

For all of the resilience routines which follow, do your best to let go of the "shoulds." Do your routines because they give you strength, keep you healthy, serve your community and other positive reasons.

Realistic Optimism

Resilient people are often described as "realistic optimists": that means that they face reality. They are the kind of people who don't put off going to the doctor or forecasting their budget, just because the news might be bad. It also means that no matter what happens, even if the news is very bad, they hold onto hope; people with mental and spiritual strength don't give in to denial or despair.

But, all of this is especially difficult when something as big as a pandemic strikes, especially if it continues for months, as we expect, as of writing this.

Your stress autopilot is neither realistic nor optimistic. It is quick to assume the worst; is inflexible; is not very creative; has a bad sense of how much time is passing; is reluctant to trust; insists on thinking of everything in black-and-white terms. Those people who hoarded far more supplies than they needed at the beginning of the pandemic, their stress autopilots, fearful for survival, were telling them to do that. Operating in survival mode is good for short-term coping with emergencies, but it is not good if that's how you are *always* functioning.

You don't want to shut off your autopilot altogether (and, you really can't). You want your autopilot to wake up as your ally when you need it, and to calm down when you don't.

Quieting it is the hard part. You can't reason with your autopilot; it isn't logical. You must *show* it, through regular experiences – resilience routines – that it is safe for it to relax, so that you can recover from stress, rebuild, and grow stronger. The good side of this is that because your autopilot isn't logical, you *can* successfully convince it that it is safe to stand down.

The resilience routines in the next few chapters will help to deactivate your autopilot, so that you can "rest and digest," "tend and befriend," and "pause and plan" more. These kinds of routines are important because, as the last chapter mentioned, your stress autopilot is sticky – the more intensely or the longer it is activated, the stickier it becomes. The pandemic is making everyone's stress autopilot very, very sticky; it is more important than ever to learn and practice resilience routines which activate your natural recovery reactions.

Realistic optimism means holding two conflicting ideas in your mind at the same time. It is realistic to acknowledge that the pandemic is a catastrophe, and that people are suffering and dying. It is also optimistic to be grateful for what's going well, and to remember that this is temporary; things will get better again. But, one doesn't cancel out the other; seeing grim reality doesn't have to erase hope, and hope doesn't make the reality go away. Inviting conflicting thoughts and feelings to co-exist is a key to surviving and thriving, because all-or-nothing, black-and-white thinking is driven by your stress autopilot – the "monkey mind" – and not your true, rational self. "Cancel culture" is an unfortunate example of this kind of stress-led behavior.

Gratitude and Generosity

Want some rocket fuel for your resilience routines? Try gratitude and generosity.

By turning your attention to what you have, gratitude reassures your stress autopilot that you have what you need – or, at least some of what you need. Generosity shows it that you also have enough to share!

Shortages are an inevitable consequence of a pandemic; as people become sick, products and services are interrupted. The problem is aggravated when people hoard more supplies than they really need, as we all learned when toilet paper became hard to find (remember, that was the "selfish and survivalist" reaction of some people's "monkey minds" taking over).

Your brain will tend to focus on what you don't have, so it is especially helpful during a disaster to take some time to remind yourself of what you are grateful for. Here are two ways to help yourself get into the habit of gratitude and generosity - try one, or both, as you continue reading this book:

Keep a gratitude diary:

You can do this daily, weekly, or somewhere in between. Write down three to five things for which you are grateful. It doesn't matter if they are small *(the store had carrots today)* or huge *(my cancer test came back negative)* – making them specific and personal is better than more general ones. What are you grateful for, about yourself? The entire point of this routine is to *notice* what you are grateful for, making gratitude into a habit. Try an internet search of *"gratitude journal prompts"* to get ideas.

Sharing your gratitude can help other people maintain their spirits, too. Just, don't ever pretend that because there are things to be grateful for, we're not also suffering; once again, it's not either/or, it's both/and.

Daily acts of kindness:

Generosity connects us to others, while building faith that we have enough. Take a moment to do something kind for someone. This has the greatest effect upon you when it is anonymous but, these days, volunteering in any way which will help to cope with or end the pandemic will benefit you, at least as much as others. As with the gratitude routine, these gestures can be small or big.

Keep Track

No matter what kind of resilience routine you choose to do, it will be more effective if you keep track. Whether it is exercise, diet, meeting with friends or mentors, or setting aside time to review your priorities, keeping a record helps. Aim for consistency. Look for long-term, rather than short-term, progress. And, look for progress, not perfection.

Technology has given us all sorts of gadgets for tracking steps, food, meetings, goals and so forth. Those can be helpful, but a pen and paper work, too.

Chapter 4:

Physical Strength and Resilience

Reminder: Your physical stress reaction is "fight or flight." When you integrate physical stress (exercise) and recovery ("rest and digest"), you become stronger at doing things.

Physical strengthening is the most familiar "stress into strength" formula, because nearly everyone understands that regular intervals of exercise, rest and nourishment build strong muscles and bones. In this chapter, you'll learn about simple, physical ways to quiet your stress autopilot and get your recovery hormones flowing, through breathing, directing your attention, and connecting better with your body and the material world.

Your Body

Covid-19 demands a *fight-or-flight* response from us as a species. We are fighting it with medical care and fleeing it through disinfection, barriers, and physical distancing. This is the right thing to do. Viruses attack our bodies, so building physical strength and endurance is also very important right now; exercise, diet, and rest matter now more than ever. Regular exercise has multiple benefits:

- It strengthens your immune system, which a stuck stress reaction wears down;
- Exercise reduces your autopilot's sensitivity and stickiness, so stress hormone levels drop;
- Your resting heart rate and blood pressure drop, and don't spike as high during stress;
- Exercise "turns on" genes in the brain which increase resilience;
- Regular exercise fights inflammation.

These days, with gyms closed and other restrictions, your exercise may not be what it used to be – but, it is more important than ever. Going outside, while keeping a hygienic distance, is safe. Go for walks and runs; take your dogs out. There's even evidence that sunlight helps to reduce viral illnesses!

But, as always, don't overdo it. *Start small; start over.* Don't worry about "sticking with" exercise; just commit to starting over, as needed. It's no big deal to fall out of the habit and begin again. Remember that you are managing your energy, not your time. Look for progress, not perfection.

Whatever kind of exercise you do, figure out the best amount and interval for you. Daily walks of thirty minutes? Run every other day for forty-five minutes? What works for you? There are many online resources which can help you figure out what's best for your age and fitness.

Temporarily denying yourself physical needs – intermittent fasting, silence and even cold showers – have also been shown build strength and health. Although some of us will say "No thanks" to cold showers, research shows that they can supply many of the same benefits as intense exercise!

Breathing

When your stress autopilot is active, you will tend to take shallow breaths from the chest and shoulders, instead of your belly. Relaxation breathing exercises help you to reverse this habit and send a "relax" signal directly to your nervous system. Deep, slow breathing activates your "rest and digest" response, putting you more in touch with the present, less anxious about the past, and less worried about the future.

You can find many breathing exercises online, as well as apps to guide you.

Note: when doing the following exercises, don't breathe so deeply that you become light-headed.

Belly breathing

- Comfortably lie on your back in bed, or on the floor, with a pillow under your head and knees. Or, you can sit in a chair with your shoulders, head and neck supported against the back...

- Breathe in through your nose; let your chest fill with air...
- Breathe out through your nose...
- Place one hand on your belly and the other on your chest...
- As you breathe in, feel your belly rise; as you breathe out, feel your belly lower. The hand on your belly should move more than the one on your chest...
- Take three more full, deep breaths. Breathe fully into your belly, as it rises and falls with your breath.

4-7-8 breathing

You can do this sitting or lying down.

- To start, put one hand on your belly and the other on your chest, as in belly breathing...
- Take a deep, slow breath from your belly, and silently count to 4, as you breathe in...
- Hold your breath and silently count from 1 to 7...

- Breathe out completely, as you silently count from 1 to 8. Try to get all of the air out of your lungs by the time you reach 8...
- Repeat 3 to 7 times, or until you feel calm...
- Notice how you feel when you are done.

Grounding

Taking a moment to *notice* things around you can turn down anxiety. "Grounding" helps you connect to the physical world.

Here's a method which works for many people - it's called "*5-4-3-2-1*":

- Name five things that you can see in the room with you;
- Name four things that you can feel right now;
- Name three things that you can hear right now;
- Name two things that you can smell right now (or, two things that you like the smell of);
- Name one good thing about yourself.

"Tapping" is another form of grounding; "Butterfly Hug" tapping is easy (and easy to teach children):

- Fold your arms over your chest, so that you can tap between your collarbone and shoulder…
- Let your mind drift, while you slowly tap yourself alternatively with each hand – do this for thirty seconds.

Most people find this relaxing. If you don't want what you're doing to be so obvious, you can do something similar by tapping your thighs alternatively – it works a little better if you cross your arms.

Progressive Muscle Relaxation

P.M.R. is based on the tightening of one group of muscles at a time, followed by relaxation. It helps to activate your recovery reactions, relieve excess anxiety, improve sleep and more. You can do it lying down or seated, but it works best when you choose a location free of distractions - you might even fall asleep!

Warming up with one of the previous deep breathing techniques can help to prepare you.

- While inhaling, contract a muscle group (see below) for five to ten seconds, then exhale and release the tension...
- Give yourself ten to twenty seconds to relax, then move on to the next muscle group...
- While releasing the tension, try to focus on the changes you feel when the muscle group relaxes – imagery may be helpful, such as picturing stressful feelings flowing out of your body as you relax...
- Gradually work your way up your body, contracting and relaxing muscle groups.

Here are the muscle groups which you can focus on sequentially:

- Forehead.
- Jaw.
- Neck and shoulders.
- Arms and hands.
- Buttocks.

- Legs.
- Feet.

On the internet, you can find detailed instructions and audio recordings to guide you.

Self-Connection

Practices such as yoga, Pilates, Tai Chi, and martial arts strengthen your awareness of what your body is doing, which physiologists call "interoception." The more you develop that sense, the more your stress and recovery reactions come into balance. These can be powerful, because we "store" stress in our bodies; when the stress autopilot is active, muscles tense. But, just by *noticing* that tension, you can take conscious control and relax. These practices include controlled breathing, with the associated benefits.

Even stuck at home you can learn some of these practices, from internet videos or e-books. If you feel self-conscious, realize that even firefighters are now doing regular yoga to help relax, activate recovery, and build strength, flexibility, and resilience.

Diet

Dieting doesn't have to mean following specific rules. That's not an approach which sets you up for success; rules inevitably lead to guilt or shame, which erode your self-control, backfiring. Instead, aim for "inclusive" eating; give yourself *choices*, instead of rules. It's okay to eat your favorite foods!

When your stress autopilot stays activated, your body will endure more inflammation, which is related to a number of physical and mental health issues. Sugars, other carbohydrates, and processed foods contribute to this inflammation; the Omega-3 fatty acids found in fish – especially tuna, salmon, and anchovies – help reduce inflammation.

Processed foods are mostly or entirely made from nutrients which were extracted from their sources: sugars, oils and so forth. They lack fiber which stimulates your gut and are easier to digest. However, just as an easy workout will not make you stronger, research strongly suggests that easily digested foods are less healthy, because they don't stress your digestive system enough, and don't properly feed the bacteria in your gut (which, we are learning, are also big contributors to your health, physical and mental).

Eating well is challenging when your stress autopilot is stuck, because stress hormones make you crave carbs, while confusing your sense of when you are hungry or full. In other words, a bag of potato chips or cookies may call your name loudly when the stress autopilot is sticking; meanwhile, the part of your brain which gives you motivation and self-discipline has a hard time competing for your attention. "Stress eating" is real.

Search the web for *"anti-inflammatory diet"* and you'll find quite a bit of relevant advice, but here are foods to avoid:

- Minimize highly processed foods.
- Watch out for snacks: they often have trans fats, which are bad.

- Soft drinks. A 12oz. soda can have the equivalent of 25 teaspoon-sized packs of sugar!
- Anything labeled "low-fat" or "low carb": these tend to stimulate your appetite.
- Fried foods.

Sleep

Although we don't fully understand sleep, we know we need it, and not getting enough quality sleep is associated with many health problems. Sleep lets us recover and rebuild from the stress of being awake.

With the extra stress of the pandemic, keeping a regular sleep schedule is more important. If you are stuck at home, perhaps you have more time, but if you're having trouble sleeping, that's not surprising: many of us are.

> *"Practice does not make perfect. It is practice, followed by a night of sleep, that leads to perfection."*
>
> Matthew Walker

Sleep hygiene

- Avoid stimulants (caffeine; nicotine), heavy meals, intense exercise, and emotion-charged entertainment, close to bedtime.

- Daytime naps are okay, but no more than thirty minutes.

- Get into natural light during the day and darken the room you sleep in.

- Avoid blue-tinted phone, computer, and other display devices before bedtime. If you use them, install software which automatically "warms" the screen hue as bedtime approaches.

- Establish a routine to signal your body that it is time to sleep. For example, a warm shower, aromatherapy, reading, or light stretching. Practice breathing exercises or progressive muscle relaxation, to help get ready for sleep.

- The best temperature for falling and staying asleep is 60 to 67 degrees.

- Stick to a regular sleep schedule.

- Don't watch T.V., talk on the phone or do business in bed. Make your bedroom a haven.

- Avoid substances which disrupt rapid eye movement (R.E.M.) sleep, especially after trauma: alcohol and some anti-anxiety sleep medications. Talk to your doctor about newer medications which don't interfere with R.E.M. sleep.

- Having trouble falling asleep because you are "tired and wired"? Try watching a light comedy that you have already seen several times. Focusing on something familiar helps – that's why you get so sleepy driving home, before lying awake wondering what changed!

- Let go of the pressure to sleep. Tell yourself "I'm getting into bed to rest," rather than insisting that you go straight to sleep.

- Know how much sleep you need. Do you wake up rested?

- If you think you might have a sleep disorder, start keeping a sleep diary and tell your doctor; untreated sleep apnea has serious potential consequences.

- Get enough exercise.

- Experiment! Try these techniques until you discover what works best for you.

Muscle Memory

Through practice, building "muscle memory" – for activities such as sports, dance, music and creative expression – can draw you into a "flow" state, where you become immersed in the activity, performing at your peak. In the flow state, your stress and recovery reactions are *both* activated, giving you great energy and flexibility.

Group activities (which at present are only possible for those who already live together) have been shown to be even more powerful, as we cooperate or compete. Many "muscle memory" group activities, such as singing in unison, include controlled breathing by a group, which research shows adds to all of the participants' recovery responses. The more ways that we feel we are part of a community, tribe or other group, the quieter the "monkey mind" becomes.

Nature

Even if the pandemic stops us from gathering in groups, we can still connect with nature. Research increasingly supports the benefits of getting out on a trail or other natural area; for example, twenty minutes a day in nature reduces the stress hormone cortisol. Stanford University researchers sent test subjects on walks through a natural area near campus, and others on an urban walk of the same distance. Those who spent time in nature were less likely to dwell on negative thoughts. The scientists followed this with brain scans, which showed a decrease in activity of the part of the brain responsible for the tendency to ruminate on negatives.

Gardening also connects us with nature, with the same kind of benefits and more. We know that getting your hands dirty can help your immune system; connecting with the natural world reminds us that it is normal for life to be messy – a constant interplay of birth, growth, death and decay. Bringing nature to you is also effective; adding a plant to a room certainly helps to calm its occupants.

Getting outside for part of the day, into the sunlight (while keeping a safe distance from people you don't live with), goes a long way toward helping your mind and body function at their best. Pick up some trash while you're out there; remember that small, anonymous acts of generosity go a long way.

Possessions

Hoarding of supplies has been hotly debated during the pandemic. Clearly, some people are buying excessive amounts, but for most it is hard to distinguish between preparedness and hoarding. One thing has become clear: it is *always* a good idea to have enough to get through a week or two; that's part of being physically resilient.

I teach disaster preparedness. Officially, the recommendation has generally been to prepare for 72 hours spent on your own. Yet, most of us who deal with disaster professionally have learnt that one to two weeks would be better. So, why the difference in the advice given? The answer is psychological: in the past, if we asked people to accumulate more than 72 hours of supplies, most people would feel so overwhelmed by the task – the cost; doing the shopping; finding places to store everything, etc. – that they would end up doing nothing at all; the shorter period feels more manageable. This is another example of why it works to *start small; start over.* Get 72 hours of supplies... then, another 72... then, another 72.

Managing physical things – money and possessions, for example – is part of what makes you strong. Too little and you won't have what you need; too much, or too disorganized, and you can be weighed down by them. You are likely to feel some stress if you haven't been looking at your budget, or when you consider the challenge of organizing and getting rid of things you don't need. Remember that you need not try to do it all at once. *Start small; start over.*

When it comes to money and possessions, gratitude and generosity can be difficult, but they are powerful ways to show your stress autopilot that you have the resources you need – and, faith that you will get what you need when you need it.

Cleaning your home and disinfecting surfaces is important to your physical health, but cleaning and organizing are also soothing for some people. Getting rid of things you don't need, and straightening up the rest, can help you to avoid the frustrations of losing track of important things. Furthermore, doing this as a household can help you to connect with one another, even if there is some arguing about who is supposed to be doing what!

Disconnecting

It is absolutely okay – and, helpful – to take time to just get away from all the craziness. Take a warm bath; read that escapist novel; watch that movie; play that video game; do a puzzle, or crafts, or art... Whatever you find soothing, give yourself permission to do it, without overdoing it.

Janet Childs, the director of our Bay Area Critical Incident Stress Management Team, typically closes out intense crisis interventions with this advice: "Go do something decadent for yourself, that has no socially redeeming value." Coping with crisis takes energy; sometimes, all we need is to get away and rest for a little while. When you are spending most of your time as a human *doing*, remember that you need some time as a human *being*.

Chapter 5:

Mental and Emotional Strength and Resilience

Reminder: Your social stress reaction is "defend and distance." When you integrate social stress (transparency; vulnerability) and recovery ("tend and befriend"), you become mentally and emotionally stronger.

We communicate with each other via words and much more; eye contact, tone of voice, body language and other social cues link our nervous systems together. One person's fear can spread to others, without a word being spoken. But, the same is true of confidence and calm: the presence of relaxed, caring people (and pets!) quiets your stress autopilot, while triggering your recovery reactions, triggering the release of hormones which rebuild our bodies, while urging us to connect and care for each other.

As you are out getting exercise or doing those essential activities, making eye contact, and greeting others, especially strangers, is a way for you to share your "tend and befriend" recovery response. In contrast, looking away and saying nothing is sharing your "defend and distance" reaction. Either way, each of us influences others much more than we might suspect.

Connecting with People

Social support matters immensely. We need each other. The more you give and receive support, the less sticky your stress response will be. The strong connection between resilience and social support makes sense: what could be better than knowing a community has your back? None of us can possibly deal with a pandemic alone. And, what could be worse than feeling alone – as if nobody has your back? Networked individuals and communities are more resilient, because they are better at sharing resources, such as tools, skills, and priorities. We learn from each other's struggles and triumphs.

We are under a lot of social stress right now. Some people are isolated and lonely, while others may be cooped up in close quarters with people who try their patience. We are also missing many of our normal opportunities for social comfort and support. Rituals such as weddings, sporting events, celebrations and so many others are canceled or postponed indefinitely – those were important.

But, even though we may not be able to travel and meet face-to-face, we still can talk to, teach, guide, lean on and support one another – and we need to, more than ever.

We are the first people ever to go through a pandemic with the internet, which is surely a huge advantage, despite its ability to spread rumors, gossip, and outrage. One of the good things which can come out of this bad situation is the development and discovery of effective ways to use technology, for more than just getting work done. Try new things! Use a conferencing app to talk to the people you would normally see in person; if you are a churchgoer, perhaps your congregation is offering digital services and coffee hours. This is a time to experiment, while also helping the technologically challenged, so that they are not so isolated.

A potential benefit of being stuck in the house comes from sharing meals more often. The simple act of eating together goes well beyond whatever words are being spoken. Eye contact, tone of voice, facial expressions, and even exercising chewing muscles together can calm everyone's stress autopilots, while triggering recovery responses. Looking others in the eye and touching sends a message that it is safe to relax, recover and rebuild. That is surely why we consider it polite to greet people by looking them in the eye and shaking hands. With the people that you can still safely touch, hugging, eating together and speaking in calm tones can all cause your nervous systems to exchange calming messages, triggering flow of oxytocin and other recovery hormones.

During a crisis, we have a greater need for people we can "get real" with. To reassure the "monkey mind" that we really aren't the only ones struggling, and that we don't have to face the pandemic alone, we need to see others and be seen; to hear them and be heard, just as we really are:

strengths and weaknesses; successes and struggles. Supportive people are the ones who listen – really listen – without judgment, and keep those conversations confidential. Without that kind of connection our stress autopilot activates because it feels alone, separated from the tribe. Exercising your social "muscles" means experiencing the stresses of allowing trusted companions to see you as you are, and accepting feedback that you may deny or dislike. Like a tough physical workout, self-disclosure and feedback spoken in kindness can be difficult – painful, even – yet helpful at the same time. This means being vulnerable, which we often see as courageous in other people, but a weakness in ourselves. Remember, this is courage in yourself. When you let down your guard and accept accurate feedback, which makes you uncomfortable or defensive, that is the kind of social stress that becomes strength.

"When a man or woman is truly honest, it is virtually impossible to insult them personally."

Brennan Manning

Although it helps to talk when we are struggling, all of us need freedom to choose *when* to talk about our struggles and *who* to talk to. Trust does not happen overnight, and "getting real" with people can be overwhelming. Give yourself and others plenty of room and patience. Take it slow.

When you offer social support, take your time before speaking. When you notice you are in a rush to speak, come back to the present and really *listen*. If you notice that you speak the moment the other finishes (or sooner, interrupting), that is much more likely to be your stress autopilot *reacting*, rather than your true self *responding*.

Are your social interactions mostly complaints, gossip, insults or your being disagreeable? Instead, aim for "daring and delightful," in the words of Sakyong Mipham, author of *The Lost Art of Conversation.* Bring "fierce affection" and "genuine curiosity," suggests Susan Scott, author of *Fierce Conversations.* Learning to stay present in conversations means developing a greater respect for your own words, as well as those of others. With practice, you will become better at this. Giving social support is mostly about being present and listening, without judgment.

Here are some ways to avoid getting it wrong:

When we acknowledge each other's reactions to difficulties, we activate our "tend and befriend" responses, deepening relationships and building mental and emotional strength. However, if you cross the line from simple acknowledgment ("that's really hard") into fixing, shaming, rejection or intimidation ("you *should* —"), that is the social equivalent of dropping too much weight on a friend who is doing bench presses. It is never your job to make others feel guilty or ashamed - this is a big, ugly myth, and easy to fall into. Although guilt and shame are useful reminders that we're doing something wrong, they are terrible motivators. They are autopilot activators, raising anxiety and robbing us of focus and willpower, encouraging distractions and procrastination. Relief from guilt and shame, in the form of *unconditional acceptance* (which is not the same as approval), unlocks the door to self-improvement; it is the difference between "you did a bad thing" and "you are a bad person." Good people do bad things sometimes. You are not what you do.

Never push, poke, or prod others into talking about painful or difficult topics. Invitations are okay; pressure is not. Recognize that trust is often tremendously difficult after trauma, and pressuring others to talk is likely to push them toward shame's accomplices: silence and secrecy. Patience and compassion, not coercion and pressure, are what makes social support work its magic.

> *"We resent being talked to. We'd rather be talked with."*
>
> Susan Scott

Empathy connects you to others; it says: "I know that feeling, too." Empathy doesn't require understanding. Even though you may not understand – in fact, you cannot – what another is going through, you can acknowledge the feeling: "that must be awful" shows empathy.

In some parts of the world, when there is a death, rather than saying "I'm sorry," or another sympathetic cliché, people say: "I stand beside you." Empathy means you are accompanying, without falling into pity, judgment, fixing or other behaviors which distance you from another's pain. Sympathy isn't helpful. It isn't quite as distancing as pity, but sympathy fails to connect us. It says: "Oh, you poor thing," expressing concern that something bad has happened, but does not demonstrate "me, too".

Don't try to fix other people, or allow them to try and fix you; watch out for *prescriptive* words like "should," "ought to" and "need to." Trying to change another person's behavior is a put-down: it implies that they are not acceptable as they are. This doesn't mean people aren't responsible for their bad behavior; boundaries and consequences are fine, as long as your intention is not to try and change them.

Resist the temptation to solve others' problems: that's like lifting their weights for them at the gym; it weakens them and leaves you too tired to take care of yourself. This is especially difficult for men. Watch Jason Headley's wonderfully true and hilarious two-minute YouTube video: *It's Not About the Nail.*

"Those who have a strong sense of love and belonging have the courage to be imperfect."

Brené Brown

Social belonging is the opposite of "fitting in." We can only know that we truly *belong* when we let go of whatever we pretend to be. Social support only works when we connect based on who we truly *are*, rather than who we pretend to be, what we do, or what we have done.

Choose your Information Sources

When we face threats and uncertainty, our brains become hungry for information – that helps us to survive. But, don't listen to everyone. Rumors will continue, which can add to your worries, as you wonder who and what to believe. Decide which sources *you* are going to trust.

Although the internet spreads fake news and gossip, it also has the unprecedented ability to connect you directly with sources of authoritative information. Turning off or ignoring unreliable sources may be difficult, because it is normal to crave information when stressed by uncertainty, but it is a smart strategy, especially for children, who need calm facts. Negative voices are always louder, including those in our own heads, but that doesn't mean they must be obeyed. Take breaks from the news and social media. The urge to learn more is very strong, so you might have to physically separate yourself from the devices calling for your attention; take a walk without your phone, and/or choose specific hours for catching up. The picture of the world you get from those whose priority is to hold your attention is rarely accurate. Keep this in mind: for every attention-gaining, scary or outrageously bad thing you see on T.V. or in social media, thousands of good things are also going on, invisibly. Take the bad news with a grain of salt. Choose who you trust.

I stopped watching television news in the spring of 2004. I know the news business inside and outside, having worked as a journalist for about a decade, primarily in radio and print, but also some television, too. I know that there are still good reporters, but in the for-profit news industry, especially television, those who don't contribute to the financial bottom line are less likely to be promoted and the first to be laid off. The result is that, slowly but surely, for-profit, advertising-based media has become about attention, more than anything else. Entertaining and enraging people are more effective attention-grabbers than informing them, so they are becoming the default.

Disconnect from your outrage. Facebook has a wonderful feature which lets you "snooze" people, pages or groups for thirty days. When you read something which leaves you feeling as though you *must* correct or convince the author, *use the snooze!* If you consistently react that way to someone's postings, it's probably time to use the "Unfollow" feature, so that you never see anything from them again. Social media thrives, financially, on your attention and engagement; it doesn't care whether it is good for you or not. Notice what emotions it is provoking in you, and exercise your choice about who and what gets your attention. Keep in mind that when you feel the urge to attack, defend and explain, that's a stress response – easily activated, but harder to turn off.

Use the snooze!

When I became a fire chaplain, I decided that I would either narrow down my Facebook friends to the people I was closest to, or open up more widely. I decided to open up, which made me realize that I needed to shut up about politics and other controversial subjects; I didn't want people to avoid me as a chaplain because of assumptions about my political beliefs, or alienate them through bickering. A wonderful thing then happened: I stopped seeing nearly as many political postings (though, this was also due to snoozing certain people and occasionally unfollowing).

Now, a few years down the road, it is far, far easier for me to resist "correcting" and bickering. This has also given me a healthier perspective: politics is important, but not nearly as important as our online arguments suggest. I remind myself to pay attention to opinions only when they come from people who really know the subject, which means also that I don't think nearly as highly of *my own* opinions (on most topics) as I used to.

I get a lot of information from links that friends post to Twitter – it is fairly reliable, because I am quite selective about who I follow. As with Facebook, I discount opinions from people who don't have any particular expertise or experience in what they write about. If they stir up my sense of outrage, I stop following them.

Not taking yourself too seriously – your opinions, thoughts, and feelings – makes a difference. I've mostly extracted myself from the temptation to comment on politics in social media, by reminding myself that I'm just one voter, without any special knowledge about 99% of the topics people fight about. These days, even *I* don't even care much what I think about many subjects! When I do have some expertise, I'll do my best to speak up, as objectively as possible, letting go of any expectation of changing anyone else's mind. If they do, great, but I'm not going to insist. Outrage – that self-righteous feeling: *"You are wrong and must be corrected!"* – is habit-forming.

When your stress autopilot activates, your brain shifts into black-and-white thinking, fueled by strong emotions. Your "monkey mind," detecting something that *feels* wrong, screeches: "Make it stop!" Bang: you're fighting, defending, attacking, and stubbornly insisting that you are right, and (more importantly to your monkey mind) the other person (or group) is wrong, and must be corrected, now!

Meanwhile, another group is quite happy that you keep going back, again and again, to those irritating posts: the owners and advertisers, who make money from your social media engagement.

Disengage. Disengage from those who provoke outrage. Step back, take a deep breath and notice who's in charge. Do you – the *true* you – really want to argue in this way? Probably not. Acknowledging where the urge comes from – a stress reaction – goes a long way toward settling your "monkey mind."

Humor

When I meet children during high stress and trauma, I often give out *"Junior Firefighter"* badge stickers – kids love them. Their parents are usually around, so as I give the children badges, I sometimes say: "This will get you out of speeding tickets!" Everybody usually laughs and some of the tension melts away. Humor helps. It helps us regain lost perspective and take a break from negativity and darkness, even at the worst of times, when used appropriately.

I'm not suggesting that you turn off your sensitivity during suffering; black humor is common in public safety, but it belongs behind our own closed doors. As a former Marine told me, "Dark humor is like clean drinking water: not everybody gets it." The risk of dark humor is that it feeds cynicism, an enemy of optimism.

Humor bonds friendships and marriages, helping us laugh at ourselves and whatever life might toss at us; silliness has the power to balance some of life's seriousness. Flexibility is a trait of resilient people. What could be more flexible than to laugh in the face of trauma?

My friend Dave, who lost a child to a brain tumor, then later developed one himself (totally unrelated; just an awful coincidence), rarely lost his sense of humor. Some of the "tumor humor" was dark, even morbid. On his brain surgery, Dave would joke: "I needed that like I needed a hole in the head;" "I gave those doctors a piece of my mind;"

and so on. Laugh at yourself, too. All of us are a bit ridiculous; it's okay to laugh now and then.

Companion Animals

Growing scientific evidence supports what we already knew in our hearts: the unconditional love of companion animals reminds us that we are not alone, and helps us to cope; dogs and horses are especially sensitive to our emotions and state of mind. Eye contact, body language, touch and other interactions raise the levels of "tend and befriend" and other recovery hormones, in pets and people.

Dogs can always tell when you've had a difficult day. Since they can't talk, they won't try to change you or make you feel better. They don't cry; they just accompany you; even though they can tell you are upset; they don't take on your feelings. That's a wonderful example of social support: dogs *accept* us, just as we are.

Horses are smart and social, incredibly attuned to our state of mind. Equine therapy and coaching show impressive results and are worth looking into, if you like horses and can imagine that they would help you.

Pets who need regular exercise help motivate us to do the same, giving us purpose and responsibility, and satisfying some of our deep need for meaning.

Chapter 6:

Spiritual Strength and Resilience

Reminder: Your spiritual stress reaction is "selfish and survivalist." When you integrate spiritual stress (struggle with values and ethics) and recovery ("pause and plan"), your priorities and purpose become stronger.

Your stress autopilot doesn't care about the long term or the big picture. It will urge you to cut corners, hurry up, abandon your principles, and even betray people you care about. Stress activation alters your sense of time: everything seems to go by much faster or much slower. When your autopilot is in charge, it may not even occur to you to consider the effects your actions might have in the long run, or on anybody outside your family and your "tribe". When confronted by an extreme threat, your own survival can become the only thing that matters.

Spiritual recovery helps to restore your normal sense of time – your normal perspective – which includes the bigger picture: your plans and considerations for the long term. It turns off the "tunnel vision," helping you to focus during strong stress responses.

Taking time to consider your priorities and set goals – even small, arbitrary goals – can go a long way toward coping with the "cabin fever" of being sheltered in place. Goals ward off boredom, which creates the spiritual stress of meaninglessness.

Contemplative Practices

Whether you call it prayer, meditation, mindfulness, unplugging, retreat, journaling or another word, contemplative practices help settle down your "monkey mind," which drives anxiety from your past and worries about your future. Learning to stay more in the here and now lowers the volume of those messages. These kinds of habits help you to be more fully present, more of the time.

Here is another way to understand that. People will say: "I'm bad at meditation; my thoughts keep drifting away." That's wrong; they are actually *good* at it, because that's the very "muscle" which meditation strengthens: the habit of noticing that you have detached from the present, then bringing yourself back into the moment.

To be resilient and safe during a disaster, it is important to regularly step back and look at the bigger picture. Public safety workers are taught to regularly re-assess emergency situations, to see if they are still safe, take note of whether what they are doing is effective, and determine if the situation has changed, so that they can adjust their actions accordingly. That's a good idea for all of us. Take breaks during the day, but also take big breaks: days off, when you really can have a chance to unwind and activate your recovery reactions. Downtime lets your "tunnel vision" expand, allowing you to re-assess your priorities and goals, based on the big picture, instead of just whichever crisis is grabbing your attention from moment to moment.

Your calendar and bank account give clues to what your priorities really are. Take a look at them, to see where you are investing your time, energy, and resources. Are those still the right priorities now that a pandemic is transforming the world? Do they reflect what you – the *true* you – really believe is important?

As I write this book, I'm struggling with my priorities, and somewhat dreading a phone call from one of the organizations I do medical work for, asking me to respond to the front lines. I'm conflicted; I'd like to stay home with my wife, dogs, and parrot, taking care of each other. My younger sister died in the H1N1 pandemic that began in 2009. Both of my surviving siblings have serious health issues. *(Update – my sister Susie lost her battle with ovarian cancer after I completed this book.)* But, I would also have a hard time saying "no," knowing that my colleagues are out there. And, we need the income; the teaching and routine emergency medical work I do are shut down.

These kinds of questions demand that each of us take some time to disengage and consider why we make the choices we do. That's what separates humans from the rest of creation: we get to choose our priorities; our purpose. As a religious person, I also ask God: "Where are you calling me?"

Mindfulness has gotten a lot of attention lately, which is good, as long as it stays in perspective. Mindfulness and other contemplative practices are just one part of building resilience and strength. They help you to do something which you may have noticed is a recurring theme in this book: to *notice* what's going on within your mind and body, so that you become more aware of when you are reacting to the past, or anticipating the future.

Remember that your stress autopilot, the monkey mind, is all about the past and the future; the dark aspects are the anxiety and worry that it creates. The good side is that it is always trying to learn from the past and better prepare for the future. When you ruminate (keep thinking about a bad thing that happened), your brain is replaying the past, so that you can learn from it. Even though you can't change the past, your brain knows that you can change the future, so it is also rehearsing, in case a similar bad thing happens again. Our brain's ability to replay the past and rehearse for the future has made us better survivors.

Contemplative practices can help keep you from getting stuck in "replay and rehearse," by developing your ability to notice when it is happening, then to acknowledge and accept it. That makes it much easier to let go.

Unenforceable Rules and Forgiveness

Frederic Luskin, author of *Forgive for Good*, describes what happens when we allow a "should" too much space in our heads. When you have no power over them, Luskin calls these "unenforceable rules." You will benefit from noticing your unenforceable rules and talking with trusted supporters about them.

Luskin has had extraordinary success in helping people work through seemingly unforgivable pain. Here's what he sees happening when you get stuck in a grievance:

- You take offense too personally;
- You blame the offender for how you feel;

- You create and repeat a grievance story, with you as the victim.

Forgiving can feel impossible or undeserved. If this is where you find yourself, realize that forgiveness is a *process*, not just a decision. Most importantly, *forgiveness has nothing to do with the person who hurt you.* Let go of the idea that you cannot forgive someone unless they are sorry; forgiveness is about freeing *you*, from the burden of your anger and resentments.

The *decision* to forgive is important, but it is separate from the *emotional process* of forgiveness:

- Recognize that whoever hurt you did it for reasons that are often impersonal; "Hurt people hurt people." Or, if you prefer, "If they were raised by wolves, they're gonna bite."
- Let go of blaming. Accountability is proper, but continuing to blame others for your ongoing life struggles is a trap.
- Discover that your version of the grievance story is not the whole story. Share it with a supporter – a

mentor, life coach, pastor, or therapist. Listen to what they heard you say. This is a time to ask for advice and rewrite your story.

When we let go of our unenforceable rules, we transform our pain from *betrayal* to *disappointment*. While betrayals are permanent and unacceptable, turning them into disappointments makes them temporary and enables the essential resilience trait of *acceptance*. Acceptance does not mean that you approve of what the other person did.

For those who strongly believe that forgiveness is a virtue, the *decision* to forgive can be very easy. However, emotional forgiveness can still be difficult indeed. We cannot rush emotional forgiveness, although Luskin's guidance can help.

Fourteen years passed before I was ready to even consider forgiving those responsible for the line-of-duty death of a member of my extended family. I felt like I was "supposed" to forgive right away – I'm a fire chaplain, after all. My attitude was that it was fine for God to forgive, but I didn't even want to think about it. Then, one Saturday, on a retreat, during a service of healing, I realized it was time.

I have no regrets; I won't "should" on myself, for taking so long. The people who helped me get there offered reflection, not pressure. The more I saw myself through their eyes, the more I realized how much extra weight I was carrying.

Chapter 7:

Children

There's a joke going around social media, that millions of parents are discovering everything the teacher said about their children is true! The stress of having kids at home while school is closed can be huge. You may be expected to work from home and supervise your children's education, simultaneously. That's a whole lot to take on, especially when you get few breaks.

Get outside, while keeping a hygienic distance from people you don't live with (but, don't stop giving your own children physical affection; they need it now, more than ever). Although many playgrounds are closed, to keep children from spreading the virus, the rest of outdoors is still there. Getting outside regularly, giving yourself and your children exercise, will go a long way toward calming everyone's monkey mind (which seems to *rule* teenagers, most of the time).

Don't be surprised or worried if children are more clingy than usual, withdraw, regress developmentally, return to sleeping in your bed (which is okay, temporarily), or play more aggressively: they pick up the fear, worry and anxiety that adults are feeling, even if nobody says anything. For children over ten years old, it is generally okay to give complete and honest information about what's going on, and how you are reacting (as long as you don't melt down). For the younger ones, it is generally better to protect them from the scarier aspects; reassure them that you and they are not going to die from this. Even with the small ones, it can be okay to tell them that you are feeling some fear, sadness, frustration, worry and so forth, but it is essential to also reassure them; they are picking up your feelings.

Consider turning off the T.V. news, especially if you have younger children in your household: it provokes strong emotions, and is intended to capture attention. That's not a healthy information diet for anyone, but it is particularly bad for kids, who lack the capacity to understand complex events.

Be direct when talking about difficult topics, such as: "Are you afraid that you or I might die?" If your intuition is suggesting that your child has those thoughts, they probably do; children figure out much more than we often realize. Be honest, because keeping their trust is *essential*. When the stress autopilot activates, we are naturally more suspicious and distrustful; give someone a reason not to trust you and they'll take it. It is far better to demonstrate sharing emotions – including the negative ones – than to pretend everything is normal. Your children know things are not normal – acting as if they are will only lead them to hold their reactions inside, which is not good. The feelings will eventually come out, often in difficult ways: temper tantrums, defiance and so forth.

Creating and keeping to routines, even while it seems as if the entire world changes daily, is important for you, but even more so for children. Give their less developed minds the great gift of *predictability*. The upside of sheltering in place is that you won't have to deal with separation anxiety which often happens during times of stress. Sharing meals is one of the most important routines; as mentioned earlier, eating together is a strong activator of recovery reactions

Get them involved in the preparation and clean-up, too: the more things you do as a "team," the better off everyone will be.

Younger children often process stress and trauma through play and art. Give them materials for art: drawing, painting, making things... anything creative. Go along with them, when you notice that they are acting out what's going on in the world; you will gain insight into what they are thinking and feeling, so that you can gently invite them to talk, if they are old enough to have the words, about how they are reacting. Let them speak, then reassure them that everyone will be okay, while acknowledging and normalizing feelings of fear, anger, sadness, embarrassment, relief, love, or anything else they might bring up or show.

Your household has new routines which may confuse and concern the younger ones. Invite them to help – having something to do is good for people of all ages – and explain, in a positive way, why you are doing it: "This will help to keep us from getting sick" is the main explanation to use right now. Kids are likely to ask more questions, so be prepared to explain, in simple ways, how and why our new ways of living protect us.

If, Heaven forbid, you end up going to a medical facility with your children, seeing the staff bundled up in protective clothing is probably going to be scary. Again, explain what everything is for, and how it helps to keep them safe. A *Sesame Street* fire-safety program for preschoolers does this, to help prevent preschoolers hiding from firefighters who are trying to rescue them. Kids get to try on coats, boots, helmets, and the "Darth Vader" breathing apparatus, so they know it stands for help, rather than a threat. Fred Rogers, of public television, told how when he was worried about safety, his mother would tell him: "Look for the helpers; you will always find people who are helping." Remind children that the fire department, police, ambulances, hospitals, and other emergency services are there for them, ready to help when they are needed. That is a powerful message for young children.

Chapter 8:

Past Trauma

If the stress of this pandemic is aggravating or triggering past trauma, you are having a normal reaction. Everyone carries a "backpack" of stress, and sudden, big changes and uncertainty can cause you to notice and feel the weight of old stress injuries much more than before the world changed.

People are likely to become grumpier and more irritable as the pandemic continues. Be patient with yourself and others. Take breaks; taking a moment for a deep breath is powerful. Unpack your stress backpack by talking about how you are reacting to the pandemic, with someone supportive, who will keep your conversation confidential. Be that safe person, for others to talk to. Writing in a journal can also help. The resilience routines in this book are not intended to heal trauma, but they can certainly help keep it from becoming worse.

Online support meetings are rising, rapidly. Plug into them if you are struggling, especially if your social support is limited; this is not a good time to be alone.

Therapists, counselors, and others, who would normally have office hours, are using technology to support secure, confidential sessions. It is a good idea to insist that they use that method, rather than going to an office, where clients are coming and going all day.

Chapter 9:

Grief

The pandemic is making grief much more common and complicated than during normal times. There is much to grieve, besides the deaths of those who succumb to the virus. We have lost jobs, freedoms, companionship, and health. Some of our dreams have died, as we contemplate an unknown, but clearly quite different, future.

Our "tend and befriend" reaction is amplified after loss, urging us to gather with friends and family, for rituals that are today impossible: we are unable to be with those we care about during suffering and death, when we would normally rush to be at their side. Hugs and handshakes from those we may not have seen for a while – sources of great comfort – aren't allowed.

So, how will we grieve? How do we avoid getting stuck in sadness, anger, or other grief reactions, when we cannot go through our normal rituals? The only reasonable answer is that we figure it out. We are in unknown territory.

Although pandemics have happened before, nobody has had today's technology. So, we are going to experiment, follow our intuitions and inspirations, and see what works, trying old and new ways to work through grief.

In Haiti, as I talked with earthquake survivors, I heard much frustration about grief. In their culture, important rituals happen at the cemetery, but hundreds of thousands were buried in mass graves in the countryside, and nobody knew where their loved ones ended up. People repeatedly asked me: "What do we do?" I had no answer, except to urge them to talk with their religious leaders, to decide what will work for them. When we cannot have the comfort of familiar rituals, we need to create new ones for ourselves; no outsider can do that for us.

It is always a mistake to compare your grief to someone else's. When we do that kind of "comparison stress shopping," it leads us in two possible directions. Firstly, we may minimize the other person's grief, failing to realize how hard something is hitting them. Grief is amplified by what's in a person's "stress backpack," and you probably don't know what they are carrying. Secondly, and worse for you, you may minimize your own grief when you decide that someone else's is worse. Never tell yourself that you don't have the right to feel what you feel; your grief is the worst grief, because it is *your* grief.

Stress and grief can be sneaky, hitting you or other people much harder than you would expect. Becoming aware of these can help you acknowledge, rather than minimize, your own or others' reactions. Here are some ways that happens:

- **Affiliation**: the more connections you have to another person, the stronger your reaction will be when they are suffering or die. If they work at the same place, live in the same town, or their children go to your children's school, all are connections which will bring their suffering closer to you, with the potential to amplify your reaction.
- **Identification**: this can be a difficult one to recognize. The more another person resembles you

or a person you care about, the stronger your reaction is likely to be. For example, the death of a co-worker, even if you didn't know them, can be intensely difficult, because your brain recognizes yourself in them. If a person who suffers or dies resembles your spouse or your children, that will probably hit you harder.

- **Sights, sounds, smells and calendar dates**: these can trigger stress reactions by reminding your autopilot of a past stressful event. For example, a police officer who served in Iraq felt some of the emotions of combat every time he drove past an asphalt plant which smelled like burning oil wells.

The saying *"Everybody grieves differently"* is important to keep in mind for this reason: grieving people, like all who are highly stressed, are comforted by anything which gives them greater control or predictability. If you tell someone else how they "should" grieve, you are taking away their control.

It has been said that the best we can bring to people in grief is our curiosity, specifically curiosity about how they are faring. Genuine, caring questions, which invite a grieving person to say how they are really doing, can be powerful. But, always remember to give them permission not to talk if it's not the right time for them.

Remember that, as the pandemic unfolds, everyone has some degree of grief. People may deny that the losses are bothering them, yet become irritable, angry, or sad. Grief may surface as sighing, a pounding heart, difficulty sleeping, an increased or decreased appetite, withdrawal from others, or any number of physical and behavioral changes.

Above all, when you are in grief, be gentle with yourself. And, be gentle with others, during their grief – which means everyone whose life has changed significantly, due to the pandemic: in other words, everyone. It is a time to be gentle and decent with one another.

Made in the USA
Monee, IL
05 August 2020